The Never Ending Cosmic Show

Riley T. Evans

Echoes of the Universe
and
Celestial Engineering

©.Copyright 2012, Riley T. Evans

All rights Reserved.

No part of this book may be reproduced, stored in a retrieval ststem, or transmitted by any means, electronic, mechanical, photocopying, recording or otherwise, without written permission from the author.

Published By Holon Publishing
& Collective Press

www.HolonPublishing.com
Twitter: @Holonpublishing

4001 East 3rd Street Bloomington, IN 47408

ISBN: 978-0-9853027-0-2

CONTENTS

Echoes of the Universe

Wind Flowers	5
A Gift of Light	6
Living Ain't Easy	7
The Field Trip	8
Through this Window	9
The Little Green Heron	10
Do Run Run, Cidny	11
A Medal for Valor	12
Capital Gains	13
His Mistress *(The Company Some People Keep)*	14
The Beginning of Christianity	15
Echoes from the Universe	16
There's Gotta Be Somethin' Better 'n This	17
Mangroves on the Inlet	18
The Sahara	19
The Nut Gatherers	20
A Blueprint of the Universe	21
The New House	23
Old Habits are Hard to Break	24
The Best of Company	25
Nor'eastern	26
A Haw in the Icing	27

Moving Along	28
You are to Me	29
Christ	30
Cares Better	31
The Guarantee	32
Glenda's Wish as She Lay Dying *(Elk Park, N.C.)*	33
Private World	34
On One's Passing	35
A View from Earth	36
Culinary Art	37
A Proper Thing to Do	38
A Mutual Accord	39
An Overture on Oak Street	40
Farm Things	42
Mixed Nuts	43
Pesticides	44
Something for Mingling	45
A Book I Wrote on the Shelf	47
The Odor of Money	48
Foxes in the Corn	49
The Poet and the Plumber	50
Battery "C" Power	51
Music Is	52
Inaugurating the First Woman President	53
Someone I Used to Know	54
An Inn of Leaves	55
A Portrait of DNA	56
Cosmic Dust	58
Twenty/Twenty	59
The Evening News	60
The Beautiful Twins *(Rain and Wind)*	61
Replacing the Snow	62
Stars *(The Outposts of Life)*	63
Tracking the Cosmos	64
Things that Squeak	66
Protective Custody	67
The Connecting Road	68
Aromas *(of her)*	69

A Spectrum of Color	70
Laugh Where We Must	72
Quaintly Granny and Charlie Duke	73
Chemaine *(on her way to womanhood)*	74
All this While Growing Old	75
Standards	76
Le 'Mer	77
Time and the Everglades	79
The Caretaker	81
Something from the Eaves	82
In Search Of	83
The Burgundy Dress	84
Imperfections of Love	85
The Pardon	86
Ferns 'n Things	87
Dress Rehearsal	88
Dawn	90
Boob Tube	91
Change You Can Bank On	92
Exit the Garden	93
Screws 'n Bolts	94
The Wish	95
Betti's Boutique *(dolls and things)*	96
Places for Things	97
Photographs	98
On the Boardwalk	99
The White Dwarf	100
Untitled Sleep	102
A Dream in Purgatory	103
An Inverted View	104
Blue Eyes Came Back for Me	106
A Christmas Tree Is...	107
Juice from These Grapes	108
Relatives	109
There's Poetry in Everything *(All You Need is a Rhyming Scheme)*	110
Linkage	111
Act IV, The Judgement	112
Act V, The Crucifixion, To Fetch a Trophy	113

Close Encounters	114
The Debut	115
Rituals	116
Uncle Sam	117
The New Chimney	118
Truant	119
Making Blue	120
The Spring of Gardens and War	121
Where Goes the Heart	122
Time and the Sea	123
In Preparation of Man	125
Nature's Nickelodean	127
The First Edition	128
The Canopy	129
In Search Of	130
The Fifth Dimension	131
Celestial Engineering	132
Forecast Earth	134
Genesis *(The Architect)*	135
Carving Out the Earth	137
The War on Path	138
Rainbows	139
The A B C's of Earth	140
Attending the Air Show	144
Brown Sugar and Green Tea *(things we commonly see)*	145
The Refinery	146

Celestial Engineering

The Gift	149
Keep the Changes Flowing	150
Gambling with Earth	151
Dawn of the Cosmos	152
The Never Ending Cosmic Show	153
A Copy Of	155
Someday God will Stumble Upon Our Burial Ground	157
The Residue of Egotism	158

War and Its Casualties	160
The Music of the Universe	161
A Dangerous Line of Work	162
Survival on Planet Earth	163
A Neighbor in Waiting	165
In Remembrance *(A Cloud of Evil)*	166
Warmed by the Wonders of Earth	167
An Internal Review	168

The Never Ending Cosmic Show

Poetry by
Riley T. Evans

Echoes of the Universe

Wind Flowers

The ever returning flowers of spring
overdue all winter long
slowly melts and winningly charms
the statue of the dawn

Each petal a symbol of hope
to mark the coming day
the wind moves flowers to dancing
I watch their bodies sway

Swinging and waving in cadence
bending to breeze that way
dipping and curtsying each other
as if in some child's play

Their regal heads now rippling
as up a slope they flow
flashing from moistured prisms
replacing December snow

If I had to ponder the wealth
`tween things like armies clashing
I'd gladly say it's more worth watching
a wild wind flower dancing

A Gift of Light

Expressing across the clustered sky
a favored expression from afar
probing the universe with light
opulent flickering of a star

Eternal glitter inclining downward
exploring earth to comprehend
Its first estate and orchestrate
the rise and fall of rain and wind

Naked cliffs and arid gorges
layered with primeval dust
react to rain's campaigning touch
emerging spores up thru the crust

Astral beams stir silent changes
volcanic rock once ashen gray
reflecting proof of wind and rain
the naked earth now verdant lays

Prismatic rays of flashing starlight
indifferent to a sterile night
propagating, the thread of life
clinging to cosmic streams of light

Living Ain't Easy

I saw a spider by the pool
hunting across the grass
for lunch-time meat, a bug to eat
to satisfy this lass

When from above a yellow wasp
was on the wing for food
to store the nest for future treats
to grow her hatching brood

Diving at the weaver unaware
she saw the stinger coming
and deftly countered the attack
worthy of her cunning

What followed was a sight to see
gnashing, tearing, biting
victor at last the spinner rose
the wasp was through fighting

She spun the prey in silken coon
attempting to hide her
when from the deck a lizard jumped
and ate the hungry spider

The Field Trip

Yellow and purple four-o-clocks
around the mountain grow
leopard's bane designed in dew
that never saw a hoe

Uncommon pinks outlined in red
on up the hill always
morning glory azure and white
napping during the day

Over the crest then down the grade
now in the noon day hour
we came upon an open glade
where stood the wild cornflower

Wedged nearby in timeless strata
unknown `til now alone
strange but lovely ferns unsleeping
clinging to barren stone

Crossing the meadow to the house
complex but not too rare
amber and hale we saw untilled
small daisies everywhere

In the garden spreading elder
had grown over the hoe
I don't know why I work so hard
to help these roses grow

Through This Window

As these present pages turn
and pass into antiquity
I too rotate my life
from future, present,
and past in you
yesterday I gladly remember
the rose and glove held out to me
by your cool, garden hands
your presence here is more
than I can understand
I awake in anticipation
of what you unclose in me
if there was some strange
cancellation of yourself
I and my surrounding world
would knock loudly
upon the doors of time
seeking entrance for my soul
for damned to pitious hell
would be the least of this burden
there is no more lonely
without you by my side
nor any dark place to hide
I shudder in thinking
and would cast a plea
to all the caring gods
imploring they would tender
this passing note
take care of you
you are the essence of my soul

The Little Green Heron

She did not stir an attack, yet
the shot with malice was aimed
stilling the herons wont to fly
now irreparably maimed

This will not bring the species down
heedless of a dragging wing
the need goes on in search for food
to feed the two offspring

Some things that never flew, akin
an undeveloped mind,
can't comprehend this ill design
something free is now confined

Yesterday each wing chased the sun
tomorrow, bird and feather
artless and torn, close asunder
will close out together

The wounded leave a scent to follow
her hunter plies North Slough
there will be no quarter given,
the fox knows what to do

Do Run Run, Cidny

The old dog sprung a leak
kidneys getting bad
twenty years round this ranch
is all she ever had
just blind, dumb addiction
could've run off and joined the circus
been something, had the smarts
instead of hanging out here
looking for a few good pets
and Alpo dog food
used to lace it with
beef stew gravy and chicken livers
the kids used to push her in the pool
`til they found out she liked it
seeding time she liked to rid
in the front end loader bucket
come thunder she'd cry at the door
run in and hide behind the commode
had to have her spayed
too many male dogs fighting
liked Sue Ann and the Vet, not local express
they sprayed her once with mace
after dark she'd run around the yard
barking at coons and `possums
never bit nothing but a pork chop bone
the animal control just drove in
to pick up the ole girl
gotta go check the back forty
it's getting smoky in here

A Medal for Valor

This dying isn't easy
these wounds sad war design
the fightings spreading rapidly
I wonder if I have time
to see what kind of world
I leave behind

Capital Gains

Priceless rays of sunset
dance o'er the rippling sea
waltzing atop the endless tide
a scenic post card pocket free

Ballerinas orchestrate
cheered on from terraced rows
attempted reproductions
of nature's rhythmical flow

Tranquil nights of shadowed beauty
courting daytime cares to sleep
moonlight masses restore the damned
and wounded souls in rich replete

Dancing visions of yellow gold
desires that have no end
captivating isolating
fated thoughts of anxious men

Sunrise fashions of painted clouds
rise aloft yon distant moor
wardrobed like the autumn leaves
vapor trails outline the shore

Materialistic accumulations
spurred on toward mortal greed
edificing, collecting treasures
surfeiting an unmet need

Earthen sweetness emerging spring
attesting to the tolling bell
for plastic wealth and foolish pride
cluttering the well-used road to hell

His Mistress
(The Company Some People Keep)

She flew in through the open window
snuggled in his bed, I'm told
I wondered when I tried to wake him
why he was so still and cold

The Beginning of Christianity

It was at most a generous plan
to ease the ancient burden of man
rescinding the rule of dust to dust
that life's sole fate was to death unjust

It was a noble, ambitious plan
to map a future for the soul of man
a second world, an eternal home
shaped by an architect unknown

The good news quickly spread the land
to every sect and native clan
acceptance faced surmounting odds
as the peoples clutched their alien gods

Quiet suspicion encountered the plan
rising from the tongue of man
indifference reigned with vocal distrust
"Lost are the dead, returned to dust"

Doubt with anger attacked the plan
jealous reactions followed from man
displaying the summit, of his skills
what he can't understand he swiftly kills

Echoes from the Universe

Enrapt with pristine edition, one ear set to the ground
I can hear the universe ticking in planetary sound
back to the window of unknown wonder
rolling in depths of titanic thunder
cyclonic solar swirling, twisting
sucking, pulling, sifting, oblivion
the trembling rhythm of vast vortices
spiraling bubbling on their axes
forging magic shapes from funneled masses
volcanic stars through nuclear gasses

An architect with uncrossed fingers
orchestrating the first of many
endless galaxies with worlds aplenty
through prisms of warping atmosphere
seed borne comets cross untold spheres
from time to time can't early avoid
land falling planets and asteroids
a star past earth just near enough
to solicit the start of human birth
not close at night to read or write by
yet far enough where often sleep lies

Olympian stars serve navigation
streaming light for habitation
beauty beyond the sweetest notion
the universe in endless motion
scoriac rivers cool pole to pole
linking nature, combining the whole
all culminating in just one goal
designing man from God's own soul
I hear the beginning ticking sound
the birth of heaven from this ground

There's Gotta Be Somethin' Better `n This

Two man force working hard
hating one `nother
no time `cept for despite
strengths oozing while complaining
rough to sleep any night
brain lights flashing
let the nerves ferment
cemetery's calling
rooms for rent

Mangroves on the Inlet

Stealthy limbs
entwining framing
entrapping silt
slowly claiming
sand knolls growing
linking, proclaiming
a virgin isle
in time
estating
the sound on
Liberty Bay

The Sahara

Blackened and barren the Mesa
rising atop the sand
under stagnant, arid skies
in poverty of water land
torrid, searing, the yellow sun
sends messages this way
no mercy here, no quarter
no tree will grow here today
in the sandy wilderness
beneath worn boulders brown
lizards their eyes awaiting out
for approaching sundown
cool the desert floor, alluring
the dwellers crawl outside
in quest of dew, a drop or two
to dampen their scaly hide
the search for mist goes on the night
the rattler licks his skin
the lizard rewipes his open eyes
for moisture to take in
wiry and wise this tempered lot
enduring the heat and pain
yet short on knowledge when to
come in out of the rain

The Nut Gatherers

In the forest reapers screening
over nuts, the big ones keeping
only the best for demand and supply
for making yearly Christmas pies
In the woods with winter nearing
the search for food becomes careering
blue tails flagging I saw them go
hunting nuts before the snow
whether large or just a gram
size to a squirrel doesn't mean a damn

A Blueprint of the Universe

Calculations on illuminating
this Godless empty place
estimating radiation to kindle
this black unwitnessed space

Infinite gleaming for cosmic streaming
construction of stars began
planets, moons, comets ensuing
then a suitable post for man

A proper plat for a universe
this unused wasted place
stars exporting breeding light
thru endless and timeless space

Billions of years linking, composing
success and a failure or two
ever selective, ever rejective
the force creating anew

Architectural wonders
reform this empty matter
proverbially claiming a universe
accented with a dab of flatter

Designing a state in the heavens
to house the force of man
the architect drew a blueprint
then built an innocent plan

O'er seas, rivers, and mountains
fertility wore a wedding band
with green swept fields and valleys
spanning an abundant land

Pressing onward over expansing
the sounds of summer behind
new galaxies reach beyond conception
built with an heir in mind

Erelong the sound of cannon
shattering the isle of man
engaging in war and genocide
traversing the vested land

One force employed with construction
creating worlds anew
the other openly displaying
a different point of view

The New House

Driving through a neighborhood
that promised peace and quiet
we saw a sign house for sale
so nice, the wife said, buy it
We closed the deal and moved right in
like normal people should
then set about the investigate
this peaceful neighborhood
We met the Smiths and Callahans
they all were so polite
except a man whose name was Burnt
he came on so uptight
He cussed his boss; he cussed the town
for all his rotten luck
and swore some day he'd move away
if he only had a truck
His chest he said was full of pain
and couldn't sleep at night
and doesn't matter how I try
when nothing comes out right
My God, I said, go right away
and see a doctor quick
else these pains might change the way
your body needs to tick
Reluctantly he saw the doc
the tests proved clear and fair
the doctor thought then sent him to
a church for heart repair

Old Habits are Hard to Break

Snake, you should have left sooner
slithering over the ground
pressing the grass blades down
catching the Beagle's eye
damn I knew you were a goner
when he came out of his corner
although I shouted 'no'
snapping your head in quick routine
then he broke you up
and skinned you clean
eying the meat
not fit to eat
he coiled it on the ground
went over to where he was before
and laid himself back down

The Best of Company

In a rude and calamitous world
where cash beds down with power
and greed rusts souls each hour
let me gladly go sit among the tender
the caring, forgotten old people
knowing I'm in warm, rich company
looking through their windows
at the twinkling, gleaming stars
dreaming of Christmas and children
each night in their silent years

Nor'eastern

An arctic blast that came to last
blew down on Quincey Bay
and caught the Dory by surprise
laying off Hudson's Cay
The wind came whipping with rolling waves
the engine ceased on going
I stepped back in the bar and thought
one hellava night for rowing

A Haw in the Icing

Prismatic, sparkling blue spruce trees
veiled in textured snow
cubes of light twinking, winking
on up the hill they go

A fragile wintry offering
clad so delicately sheer
diadems of polished sunlight
marking this time of year

Crystalline, surreal reflections
an annual scenic token
panoramic snow in motion
a masterpiece unspoken

Bounding stately across the snow
bolts the stag, uncloaken
a rifle quakes; the crystals break
two masterpieces broken

Moving Along

I had these nagging symptoms
on and off for years
knees and shoulders aching
and ringing in my ears
the doctors plied their needles
and gave me big white pills
nothing worked completely
I lived on with my ills
I knew I was coming down with something
just couldn't figure what stage
`til one day I saw in the mirror
I had broken out with old age

You Are to Me

What is therein so still your eyes
I do not understand
that is deeper than the roses
when I give you my hand

Unclosing this heart as spring now
petal by petal unfolds
these drifts of pale blue flag
attesting to the sun

Weaving patterns delicately
of love to last the sands
arranging here, there, with your touch
woven by such small hands

As flowers need the sun like them
this simile's too near
so winning the heart weeps fondly
paling your eyes austere

You could kill me now too swiftly
as I cannot withstand
sadness when fills your stilly eyes
quickly I give you my hand

Christ

I like this man Jesus ongoing
about his business well
cleansing sinners, catching the waste
then flushing it back to hell

Cares Better

From love's arms I fled shattered
and broken by the fall
all `twas love, love only love
and nothing else at all

I needed care sought did I care
care from the faults of love
I needed care for ugly wounds
from then and not hereof

Scarce was care, a neglected thing
like star dust in the hall
strange when I found someone who cared
I had grown a bit more tall

The Guarantee

Assist me in this quest to know
no witness to the silent change
from birth of crusted rocks ill strewn
coursing Earth's sulfuric range

What architect designed and assigned
introductory shapes of verdant stands
overcoming lava, threading rills
evolving patterns mold the cooling land

In this primary wilderness
before the shadow seen of man
twisting rivers rippling tides
spawn the bloom of newly formed land

Pristine pools and mirrored streams
publicize raw, fertile fields
linking sunlight, soil, and water
vital to affluent yields

Each element in the formative draft
destined to support the ultimate plan
ensuring and sharing its common wealth
cradling the birth of coming man

Night time vision issuing stars
filtering light and sleep abound
all the elements counseling man
tread softly, brother, you're on holy ground

Glenda's Wish as She Lay Dying
(Elk Park, N.C.)

Through yon window I try to imagine
as dawn draws back the drapes
a never ending encounter with
lovely changing mountain scapes

(Dawn cracking on the heels of night
and morning stars burning bright
blossoms of snow poised aplomb
adorning grand fields of autumn
the snowy owl perched encumbered
inside a day of watchful slumber
the distant clouds that dip and bend
to silent service of the wind
prisms of light where sun strikes dew
enchanting woods to ramble through
the stag breaking bold in flight
over snow in the morning light
these noble things a gift I know
from one, the master of the show)

If I could frame what's in my mind
and bring to view these August sights
and lay beside that window instead
a bed in a room without any lights

Private World

You are fair reason to note
Your eyes speak
their deepest feelings
enjoined in silence
where trembles
an act of love
when two as one
rise bearing wings
speechless
in secret to go
unencumbered in flight
o'er the beautiful snow

On One's Passing

I stay this winter on borrowed thought
I find a silent ear
I cannot see a spring with roses
So cold this time of year

This harvest of cryptic ashes
so bitter a bloom this year
adopted thought for winter solace
perched so silently here

This garden vacant of roses
the ferns wizened and sear
the sky intact in lusterless black
uncommon the clime this year

My footsteps falling on embers
echoing so crystal clear
distinct the smell of haunting dust
these thoughts I wish not hear

Arresting this winter solace
gripping in somber fear
I face the sober, vaulted ashes
that mark this solemn bier

I seek for spring to thaw these cinders
that borrow upon my ear
when time will restem the flowers
to smell her roses next year

A View From Earth

Here now I can imagine and see
an endless skyway through the stars
for celestial voyagers to mark
and navigate the galaxies afar
on a charted course
to the rim of eternity
where even now
from vortical debris
spiraling galactic nebulae
created so orderly
and when the final orbits
are fixed and spun
for new moons and planets to run
the force moves on across infinity
to light a void
with another galaxy
and sprinting from behind
with little rest
hell bent on this olympian commerce
man upon his tracking
endless quest
chasing God
across the universe

Culinary Art

Tiny, mud-lined, shoeless prints
mark these polished floors
from down the hallway backward to
a left wide open door

Her face was streaked as too the hands
in a dirt mixed shower blend
from making and baking mud pies
with abetting, wet proof friends

Crying, she said, we need a tray
cause Millie's big sister's there
and took our stuff right from us
in tones of great despair

To the bath with you she affirmed
and stay off my fresh waxed floor
wash those dirty feet, young girl
then close that swinging door

Soon spic and span with pan in hand
the chef skipped out the door
it won't take long to look just like
the way she did before

Reshining the tile you could see
a gleam in her eyes so plain
gladly Mom would never love someone
that did not like the rain

A Proper Thing to Do

Stiff were your words and unkind
not having more sway with me
pouting defiant entreating
a trip across my knee
Had the door been worn to weather
instead of new and stout
chances are it couldn't withstand
that slam when you went out
Clumsily with a wooden sword
you slew a yellow rose
stabbed some mums, then fixed the jasmine
where they'll never close
The cat was napping but one had thought
to be awake was better
so pulled his tail then turned the hose
upon the Irish setter
God, how welcome the still of night
when would-be knights need sleep
before I went that way myself
I thought to check my keep
This is not the dragon slayer
that smart lipped off at me
no, this is not he, but some dear
other personality
It's most unusual to learn
angels can change their faces
and when they tire, some tend to sleep
in the damnedest of places
I could not comprehend just then
which little boy I knew
but cheered by what hadn't changed
this care for both of you.

A Mutual Accord

Flightless over the windrowed field
bent winged we saw him go
where the meadow pulls up sharply
to let the forest grow

I followed to the wooded edge
intent on some repairs
to much surprise with mended wings
he left the ground by air

I wisely thought there was a scene
he tricked someone to see
the gaze around was casual
until there was this tree

Strong built on several branches
were nests of twigs and string
when above the peeping cheeping
you could hear the trickster sing

Never was heard such shameless singing
but oh the courage there
it was then I knew he had me
damn, this isn't fair

I think he likes the way we've let
this woodland grow ax free
and now hell bent on keeping me
co-owner of his tree

Straight forward to the house I went
with a grandiose design
found paint and brush then painted not
across this for sale sign

An Overture on Oak Street

Inside the swale along Oak Street
where stood the water ankle deep
a small, barefoot, mud streaked lass
was wading and splashing in the grass

Fine rain was lightly falling down
matting her hair as too the gown
when suddenly she stopped and took
at the manor a long, hard look

Behind locked doors now safe inside
an elder lady rose and spied
on the rumpled girl at play
stirring thoughts of yesterday

Oh, to be that age again
agile, young, but not that thin
to once more feel the pat of rain
while limping with a twisted cane

The little waif approached the house
quieter than a Christmas mouse
pressing her face against the pane
while gran dame gazed out at the rain

She stared transfixed into the room
forgetting now this outer gloom
at all the golden bric-a-brac
and fine clothes upon a rack

Oh, to be that rich and warm
instead of cold tattered torn
then backed away to shrug a sigh
the woman bent and caught her eye

They watched each other for a while
then broke the silence with a smile
how warm the glow was like a torch
they compromised and sat on the porch

Neither one was quite aware
as they sat visiting there

friendship has no special inning
it only needs a little beginning

Farm Things

Beyond the lawn spread near the corn field
cow egrets grazing
for what moved or was secreted in low grasses
the morning sun
took full a picture of the tranquil feeding
when breaking full speed o'er the meadow
a black dog ran `em off
`round noon the cattle watering hole
three blue herons
working the banks for minnows and frogs
when the black dog
in a flurry ran `em off barking
in shadows of evening sunset, grackles
grubbing just made flight
as the fur raised dog ran `em off
dawn broke, rose, I rose swiftly, rose and
ran the damn dog off

Mixed Nuts

The eulogy was over and
the coffin lowered down
people feigned in crying while
the preacher moved around

I don't know why they dressed in black
lamenting soft and low
when most were touched with gladness
to see the bastard so

Pesticides

The crap they sprayed on the insects
passed through each body wall
went on down to the water line
pumped back to kill us all

Something for Mingling

It is that time when shadows
have quietly lost their stay
now moonshine girds their descendants
in yellow, soft array

And there where the falling water breaks
two naked pines display
their likeness over the waterfall
as swiftly it churns away

Here, the legend of Arethuse,
is where she was reborn
from fairest of fair young maidens
to water one early morn

The ancient curse of Alpheus
cloaks me not in fear
that drowning be the penalty
whoever trespass here

Hard sculling the awkward dory
away from the rocky shore
in search of the fabled lovers
in doubt of aged lore

Out on the river of legend
far from the tree-lined shore
Alpheus and Arethuse mingling
likened to Grecian lore

A spray went up from the channel
the boat rode a seaward bore
mist eclipsing strange moon light
losing sight of the shore

Tossing, turning the long boat ran
down the river screaming
the hull rode out the starless night
as if I were in dreaming

Out where entangling seaweeds
wreathe an open door

down through the dangling sargasso
down to the ocean floor

Wakened by daylight to seaward
clutching a sculling oar
no longer in dream I'm dreaming
doubting no more this lore

A Book I Wrote On the Shelf

Drawing from their thoughts this script
the tender I met each mile
the gentle, the kind that made them wise
feeling taller in their smile

They go now among these pages
in silence lettered to dwell
their touch, their work never over
they read from here too well

The warm, the sage amid these pages
I envy to almost sin
so if I make a name for myself,
maybe they'll let me in

The Odor of Money

The naked freedom of innocent birth
such moments of childhood finger delight
when wonders spring out thru gentle eyes
that tell the arms to cuddle tight

Proceeding on inquisitive tip toe
thru time when boy grows into man
then mingles with monetary strangers
unknowingly becoming an ardent fan

Valuing worldly possessions
palaces bejeweled in ornate style
filled with materialistic matter
soft gods amassing pile upon pile

Conflicting with man's rightful nature
to copy the shepherd and shield the sheep
money derailed a sovereign trust
now his castles intend to keep

Fortunes speed from dubious places
where false idols are framed to adore
God, accept our selfish weakness
when we least agree with you more

Foxes in the Corn

Meeting first in time on the meadow
stiff with new suspicion
we passed each other
she to feed new kittens
I to hoe weeds in the corn
on the path when after
we met yet did not cross
but stood at ease eying each other
the vixen with a brown hare
limp between her jaws
me with a hoe across the back
then with mutual animal grace
we passed aside each other
not owing up to fear

Time an ally of affinity
the fox would enter the garden lot
with a cocked head expression
(absent of any scorn)
and look as if she really liked
the way I hoed the corn
spring ran into early summer
without an inkling of fear
the kittens played in the rows
although I tilled there near
summer gave way to autumn
the pups grew and romped
the fodder corn reached upward
and tasseled with regal pomp

Now autumn is gone; the cubs are grown
I watch from over the field
as two red coats they go
learning to hunt before the snow
she off to the hills for a little sin
find her mate get pregnant again
in a world deaf to peaceful negotiations
where treaties are made then broken
This, this accord went down
without a single word being spoken

The Poet and the Plumber

The plumber cautiously
reaming the pipe line
to open the kitchen drain
The Poet carefully
choosing words to explain
the opening of flowers
Both good at what they do

Battery "C" Power

I saw a little, fuzzy worm
struggling under attack
by a red horde of frenzied ants
not liking the odds, that's a fact

I quickly found the insect spray
and shot the mobsters dead
hoping to spare the victim who
was fixed to lose his head

When the bummers quit their shaking
I brushed them from his hair
and with my finger gave it a push
to go and breathe some air

He lay unmoved; it didn't look good
he was not up to go
I nudged him again and again
but still it was a no

Looking perplexed sensing dread
verging on giving up
when the mechanic's kid down the street
came by with a slurpy cup

He asked me if I was feeling right
I told him of the problem
he felt the worm that didn't squirm
stepped back and said Ahem

He fumbled in his pocket `til
he came up with a buzzer
hooked one end to his radio set
the other end to fuzzer

Then held the button on until
the worm crawled up a stem
looked at me grinned and said, first
you gotta jump start him

Music Is

Music is love
looking for words to explain
the trickle, the sound
of falling rain
the patter against
your window pane
the bending of grass
across a plain
the aching of hearts
in separate pain
purchased lips
that kissed in vain
the rustle of leaves
among the grain
you and I
trying to reclaim
a love that started
in the rain

Inaugurating the First Woman President

This occasion asks our past indifferences to scold us
and seals this blessing with new hope that stirs
the heart to hear again the wisdom of Athena.

The generations we lived in slumber when women were
bought and sold, graded to wives, trusted to vote and
clean the toilet bowl, are left now to the pages of history.

Whether you're from Adam's rid, heaven, or disturbed
parents, we hail you now "the Chief"
God have mercy on skeptics souls

Someone I Used to Know

I dread not now my first gray hair
but in this late spring, prize
Time; time so short I find no room to
reminisce nor memorize

The clock allowing this chance for me
to tell you oft, to know
you dance like the beautiful go
by your leave, I say it's so

An Inn of Leaves

Sun bitten with perspiring brows
tilling the land in trade
the farmhands sought the one lone oak
in need of cool and shade

Overhead in steady numbers
feathered guests with no regard
checking in and checking out
for cash or credit card

As air waves ring of mocking birds
and blue jays that chatter
gray flagged squirrels juggle nuts
heedless to this natter

Tender abstracting music
breaking upon the day
from golden throated orioles
sole in the clime of May

Approaching the wagon, I
in awe at what I see,
then fueled by some human need
to hug myself a tree

A Portrait of DNA

Surgical beams of spawning starlight
probing shores on sea-girt ground
birthing in auditory strains of life
as the ages passed, cooling down

Beginning blocks of new existence
antedated helically wound
microscopic cells of matter
a plan too subtle to set down

A flash of wonder graded upright
launching in the wind to blow
fibers of cores with moot ancestry
streaming of radiance ruling it so

Under seas and over ranges
soulless spores of life swirl round
carefully seeking earthen nurseries
to let their fumbling roots run down

Yon mirror moon with cold reflection
attests the dawning motes
sprawling the warm hide of earth
cataloging envious notes

Shadows of life patchwork the planet
facing fresh worlds on windy slopes
memory is cast from rote perception
as careers on earth begin to grope

Thundering volcanic exposures
defile uncharted embryos
fragment by fragment thru raging storms
cell by cell challenged they grow

Tissue by tissue, leaf by lead
asocial dateless while ascending
the conscience thrill of life unfolding
pearls by starlight without ending

Infusing hues of incandescent light
color all living things below
red for the emerging roses

white a thing with falling snow

The perilous journey from titanic thunder
to dancing waves and earthen green
saw limbs and flesh inherit a soul
that dared to hope and quietly dream

Reacting to this comprehensive plan
the steward of fate, immortal and alone,
celebrates his creation of man
by hurling stars into the vast unknown

Cosmic Dust

A yellow cloud from up in space
new to my detection
descended slowly to the Earth
to come in my direction

Tiny specks of alien dust
enriched with golden beams
ghostly falling down the field
in ever constant streams

By eve this breeze in quaintly mode
in all points was flowing
I couldn't tell whether the wind
was coming or going

It set against the window panes
and under eaves came creeping
I settled in and loudly thought
no gentle night for sleeping

By dawn the air was clear to fair
the wind was down, near stop
I looked across the field and saw
new soil for next year's crop

Twenty/Twenty

From a distance, waylaid with beauty
by regal mountains crowned with snow
under a sizzling solar plan
yielding at sunrise, fawn and doe

Exposing pine saplings and forest fern
dyed golden by the morning light
oak leaves hanging from sleeping trees
explaining the hidden facts of night

From a distance yon waning moon
stubbornly pulls the waves ashore
strewing the beach in hillside medley
on each receding tidal bore

Seceding rocky mountain embers
wash down the precipitous land
brooked onto the sea by rivers
lie paved across the strand

From a distance yon dwindling stars
that light the roads of clumsy night
shadowed now by the rising sun
close out their Sunday guiding light

Far ranging further constellations
unseen thru the prevailing light
orbiting planets follow their stars
each has its own disguising night

From a distance our universe
is shaped in structured beauty
each broad design connecting time
by an architect's hallowed duty

An eye can see all things that grace
like roses in love with dew
but things up close like massive greed
blindside our line of view

The Evening News

A mural dangles at twilight in the western sky
painted on clouds in media's solar light
against interstellar space tumbling into eternity
where the fields are candled with endless stars
flaming color spectrums composing, changing
pageantry beauty in the vital atmosphere
windfall colored mists wing celestial arches
of rainbows streaming thru God's open hand
flamingo hues on azure blues wake wistful hearts
recalling treasured moments since long apart
and far below in the shredded October fields
attending the show an awe struck fawn and doe
the barn owl stirs with unfed hollow eyes
wondering what prey in the meadow lies
the inviting portals of night clad in quiet
open calling the weary to sleep sans light
stars begin to flicker and glimmer; the vision dims
the sun sinks below the engulfing sea
curtains of night herd the failing light
This broadcast paints for you a non-commercial view

The Beautiful Twins
(Rain and Wind)

Where goes the sailing cloud
across the lengthened sky
its valuable cargo of rain
seeking some place to lie

Athirsting fields of table grain
rescued by the passing shower
lifting each drooping, curling leaf
soothing one little angry flower

The service of the wind chauffeurs
for clouds can't pick their places
blown from east pushed from the west
exposing rainmaking faces

Nourished oaks fall tiny acorns
birds drink from little pools
the rain and wind fund life and limb
and recognized by simple fools

Clouds and friends are much the same
just dropping in with, "How do you do?"
but underneath the breezy visit
each one's concerned, thinking of you

Replacing the Snow

Twilight introduces slumber
sunrise lifts mine eyes in wonder
dare not I flirt with second sleep
the flowers awaken to my keep
with taste of sleep upon the tongue
I rise and meet the spring day sun
then watch as daybreak pulls the drapes
and opens up the valley scape
down the slopes on the fertile floor
I see among not there before
anemones of peerless white
that bloomed before the end of night
to greet and welcome, an honored duty
a land covered with timeless beauty
now in this waking, nodding hour
I dream a field of wild wind flowers

Stars
(The Outposts of Life)

Starlight rippling through the world
homing on Earth, touching down
curving, planning, estating life
transforming dust without sound

Swarming beams of fertile firelight
father breath and future hopes
the hazy march of innate seedlings
scrabble for footing on callow slopes

Petals of an unfolding age
glorify the naked hillside
proof from the amending leaves
by sifting spoils man can abide

The change that changes on this stage
converting bubbling, tainted smoke
to atmosphere ashen free
that youth may start its infant stroke

Charity by her hand unraveling
the master knot of the human race
the unshed leaves hug tight the tree
bough and tree submerged in grace

Millions of stars and unknown planets
freckle the endless universe
creation cast one cosmic process
destined starts cannot reverse

Tracking the Cosmos

From this dear and familiar place
I watch the sunlight stroke dancing leaves
then quite properly the wind moves on
quieting the balding autumn trees

Windfalls rumor the surfing shore
where waves pave the coastal land
the mystery of the moon pulling tide
avows "I am one with mountain sand"

Surging, ploughing, pounding swells
carve the strand with a sweeping hand
and shape the beach with volcanic medley
the sculpture's logic lies cast in sand

Communicating 'tween quarter moons
as shifting waves go out on the neap
shadows among the sun and earth
whisper softly, "I do well with sleep"

Changing starlight aberrations
forming in earth's stratosphere
atomic blue gas masks radiation
shielding the lower climate, "quite dear"

Along the corridors through deeper space
traveling from earth to planets afar
falling flares swirl in the darkness
as comets pass from star to star

Messenger bright celestial bodies
on generous missions to disperse
spreading arcane nucleic atoms
sharing secrets with the universe

Throughout the seamless, boundless sky
exploding in flaming cosmic gusts
dying stars deliver new worlds
from primary nuclear cycling dusts

The ultimate beauty of starry nights
lighting the way for man to wend

addressing a knowledge beyond his reason
of a universe that has no end

The vast, articulate healing waters
allow a one-time life reprieve
for man injecting carbon venom
or facing a dying, polluted sea

Life finds roots within the ocean
flesh aborts in acidic rain
to not resolve debts of the past
leaves little hope for future gain

Things that Squeak

Rusty hinges on old barn doors
new shoes the first time worn
young girls trying to reach high "C"
mice in the fodder corn

In dark moon, spooky midnight hours
branches rubbing at night
against a withered chimney flue
sending the spine in fright

Old cars grinding in need of grease
creaking roofs just at noon
quaint cane chairs that need some fixing
lots of squeaking going on

But the best, I think, are April showers
passing over the green
leaving the meadow and apple trees
a fresh and squeaky clean

Protective Custody

Weeds have a place in the garden
after harvest they hold
when ravaging winds try washing away
an earth that won't let go

Lasting against the winter winds
that bring but lifeless cold
defending soil the lowly weed
sets erosion on hold

Ornery burrs are first to appear
after the passing snow
cropping out to see if it's safe
for wild flowers to grow

The Connecting Road

Unused through the tall, eternal sky
trailing from the abyss of conception
coursing `round, over, under past worlds
nests a highway in space and time
far-reaching the open gates of eternity

Where even now from the pulsating bowl of creation
dynamic forces publish new galaxies
born from fragments of interstellar dust
while infant stars candle the voyage with celestial glow
for pilgrims to approve the cosmic beauty of the universe

(attending this circle of flickering, resplendent light
would place witness to the cardinal body of God)

Here eons of time are quiet and remotely worn
yet they undress a hunger for companion souls
a longing father looks back across the ages
anticipating the winged flight of man
but finds him inflicting terrible carnage where he can

Possessed with an unredemtive addiction to war
sadness spills over to doubtful existence
this slender road hasn't seen many travelers
only Christ has passed this way in salvage
will it be? He comes this way just once

Aromas
(of her)

These walls asleep of sweet laughter
wisps of air alluring loom
the vernal scent of earthen umbers
linger and `twine this room

Her gardens vent among these fabrics
beneath this August moon
wear my senses to ask in wonder
will she come back and soon

I feel these linens lonesomely
then swiftly do assume
she's gone; then I heard a rustle
hell, she's in the other room

A Spectrum of Color

A time for earth to build its fortune
collecting shell from cosmic scree
attracting infinite swirling hosts
and endless effects of stellar debris

The foremost reach of the universe
finds favor with the infant sphere
showering its surface with meteorites
ionizing the atmosphere

Boundaries of the earth contain
articles from an exploded sun
now cloistered in silence and darkness
completing it's farewell run

Countless shapes of galactic matter
fashion the planet's prolific crust
particles below of forgotten worlds
mix clouds with dying mineral dust

Employed in all genetic beginnings
pigments float within earth's breast
giving each set of genes identity
a gift to differ from the rest

Spawning the seeds of existence
water, sand, and solar light
when the eager roots sink down
each fiber absorbs its color birthright

Rising into a new-formed world
discretely from the celestial ground
flowers, mountains, and man from dust
pristine wonders in time abound

Graduating flowers unfolding
across the courting naked land
draping the ground in glorious color
a present of the tinting sand

Mountains push thru the planet's crust
reassembled from numbered atoms

reaching majestically for the clouds
a vision too steep to fully fathom

Ere the developing line of trees
climb up the moving mountain land
helic models of life assemble
the complex fabric of coming man

Endowed within the genetic dust
an act from God to rehearse
each man black, white, yellow, or red
the role of shepherd in the universe

Laugh Where We Must

You got on at the station of man
now fill this circle as best you can
be calm and wise reach into catastrophe
pull out some broken souls and set them free
be to them as a god as God is to thee
lead them in a direction they cannot see
teach them to shoot folly where it lies
let evil wither into sunny skies
never dress or agonize in fear
from life, for God is ever standing near
treat doubts as shadows stealing up the spine
knocking on the back door of the mind.

Quaintly Granny and Charlie Duke

Caged bird
in a cage singing
singing bird
upright and swinging
little one
she keeps a' feeding
for grain he
must be ever needing

If she lapsed and
faulted his feeding
most certain
he would be a'keeling
then she'd
stare bewildered seeing
bird on his back
feet toward the ceiling

Chemaine
(on her way to womanhood)

Sometimes earth doesn't understand the child
a struggling rose contending to bloom
inside beauty richer than all truths
upon this land will yield it's fragrance soon

Time cannot color the days to charm you
from night to night suffering craving relief
from careless barbs hurled at thy breast
while holding fast the roots of good belief

Soon precious in the April dawn you'll stand
lovelier than lilacs to be a part
of enterprising earth that needs your light
your fingers clutching God's forgiving heart

All This While Growing Old

Escaping fragrance from the yellow daffodil
embarks upon the dawning air to breathe
white and red the apple buds of April
sharpen the senses `round the nostrils weave

The lush and green prescription of summer
disorderly filed among the yellow clover
while trailing purple buds of muscadine
come upon a split rail fence and climb over

The changing brown and orange leaves of Autumn
producing varied hues left and right
wind picked defecting to the claiming dust
absent now of life-producing light

Words I could not say lay atop my tongue
from love employed with blue and gentle eyes
unsaid yet thoroughly understood
then pale into the snowy winter skies

Seasons meet with beauty everywhere
warm sunlight and rainbowed blossom
except in these gray, feathered days
memory is the last color in the spectrum

Standards

A fugitive from heights
across the field he goes
seeking solace
in the song that flows
(the yellow throat controlling silver notes)
of mournful whistling
ah, so sweet and low
that tempts the ear
and calms the fractured soul
his song perhaps
a timeless hand-me-down
when cosmic dust
consumed the fiery sun
and metaphors of night
ran with the dawn
earth in its
early, early spawn
winging never high
above the field
homing eyes fixed
on the ground
oh Meadowlark
what secret do you hold
that dooms you to
be valley bound?
eagles nesting
yon mountain crest
glare at artless
wings so slow
offensive eyes
suggesting
lark you fly
too damn low

Le `Mer

Star earth boldly unassuming
cooling, liquefying solar flame
creating an all submerging tide
to cradle life in her domain

With an uncontrollable urge
over eons designing flesh and bone
rarest of all treasured pearls
the charting seas bear life alone

Undersea figures patterned to swim
the ultimate time here now begins
opaque grasses sway anchored down
the sun warms up its extinguished kin

The first glaze of time wears thin
where waves never break nor pound
aqueous, incommunicable sea
entombed in silence tightly wound

Breaking through calm, healing waters
from the bowels of central ground
inch by inch, millennium by millennium
islands rise introducing sound

Infant coasts patrolled by water
washing o'er the sea girt land
moon attracting celestial forces
processing minute grains of sand

From the depths of a fashioning world
triumphantly breaking upon the day
great continents deep beneath the waves
majestically rise with due delay

Volcanic molten, titanic eruptions
blot out the sun for eons of time
creating tall ridges, outstretching earth
authoring script for sulfurous clime

The second layer of time begins
where waves break on the early shore

the air is sweet plumed; ash retreats
and the sun beams through a cloudless door

Petals for an unending green world
maternally impulsing from the seas
creating, duplicating from wide, wide water
flesh, bones, and ranking trees

Slowly colonizing earth with life
drawn on figures from the sea
the lands enriched with dawning shapes
climbing, grazing, flying by scant degree

Tenderly with greatest care
awash then sowing upon the sand
a need to mold from earthen clay
a being as sovereign o'er the land

Procreating pass weeds and flowers
building edifices from mountain stone
man falls in love with worldly pleasures
publicizing his comfort zone

Dreams he, dreams have no boundaries
all earth's estate he claims his own
the venomous carbon he casts in the sea
a wasteland makes what he has thrown

The third and final coat of time
begins with fated news as host
the dying ocean befouled by man
killed by the hand she loved utmost

Time and the Everglades

Northwesterly winds crisp chilling
already cool fall air
over an island, dotted land
home to kite and marsh hare

Decaying building atop itself
this peat-land slowly grows
supporting sawgrass and cattail
unnoted for a rose

Reflecting close imitations
that passed this way ago
the raw savanna wet, then sere,
home for dawn, buck, and doe

Red hawk, raccoon, silent cranes
mud hens teal, herons blue
spoonbill wrens, egrets, and bream
indwell these glade lands too

Resilient yet graceful each species
each with its own design
ranging these frangible wetlands
for one eternal time

Seasons merge with tender changes
fair weather sees the days
nobile guests lodging, the region
react in restive ways

Pushing through muck-tinted water
timeless lilies here abound
yellow pristine flowers waking
rising bravely too, around

My Lord, I'm witness here to see
living islands in this bay
and wonder-struck what rain can do
when mixed with sun and clay

Winter's wave of restless migrants
ends with an inbred bell

loons and geese summoned homeward
exclude this grand hostel

Rising stately without number
gleaming in dawn's golden light
wending over endless cities
lending Earth an awesome sight

Untold knolls commence appearing
across the shrinking glade
predawn flora e'er so fragile
begin to die and fade

Spring abruptly sows swift changes
clouds of drought scud yon air
the burning need for ample water
recedes with warmer fare

As the welcome summer rains come
thundering and crashing down
It doesn't take much wit to see
It's best to post "Keep Out All Towns"

The Caretaker

Somewhere I can imagine
the silent opening of flowers
numerically disclosing petal by petal
birth in a chambered bower

(movement along the milky way
planets circling the stars
orbits at the edge of eternity
equate the conduct of Mars)

The velvet leaves in disclosure
aroma traps the wind
where day is yet half over
when colors soon begin

(solar winds find passage around
the spiraling, whirling worlds
rounding bodies in drag relief
with every cycling twirl)

As flowers arrive, fumbling bees
practice one craft they know
passing along genetically
returning roses from the snow

(crusading comets blaze the skies
freighting pollinating dust
wherever galaxies court each other
new stars and planets adjust)

Inscribed upon these productions
where time and space are the same
keeper of the universe, author of the rose
collectively share one name

Something from the Eaves

Dead bird, yours
was the shortest flight
from egg to
hatchling you rose
tried those early
wings that failed
and fell I
swear I did not know
her cat liked
young wrens so

In Search Of

Gray dawn fingered with coming light
overhead in practice flight
soundless the great blue heron sails
on the ashen fringe of night

Broad wings stiff in power gliding
a ghostly sky dreadnought
razor-sharp, inspecting eyes
seeking prey to be caught

As dawn turns off the waning night
an osprey perched tree top
scans the canal with clever eyes
alert to make a sudden drop

Stalking the banks for bait they go
all day in quiet procession
herons, egrets, and silent cranes
plying their profession

It's hard to take time for nesting
In search of food sans rest
I guess that's why from time to time
Eggs don't hatch in some birds nest

The Burgundy Dress

I apologize not complimenting
the striking suit
I was employed with
the woman wearing it

Imperfections of Love

To understand, to see
beyond the harsh words
I could not make-believe
your venom did not hurt
(your presence unlikened to this degree)
yet this day you chose to strike
at the underpinnings
of the fabric you wove in me
(I thought at first unwell)
no, this air between us
is too thick and odorous
of armorment
no, the strike was not for me
but you trying to untangle
and trample the unseen beauty
that interlaces the soul
damned to be free
fanning the embers of hell

The Pardon

In time atop that little hill
onto the marsh they came
changing the air from musk to sweet
lilies without a name

Soon the children were found to know
when riding through the wood
their favorite place to stop and play
was where those flowers stood

Towered above that midget mound
a forest great and tall
the narrow rise was not discreet
aroma reached them all

Startled one day the birds took flight
then trees came screaming down
to build a road, huge earth machines
cut up the arum mound

Soon the memory passed away
the incident forgot
now children ride in bright, new cars
where shetlands used to trot

A splintered piece of loam remained
among the broken trees
before a golden, morning sky
uprose a pleasant breeze

Inside the path of use no more
perchance in private grace
a patch of lilies grooming the air
each had a scar on its face

Ferns `n Things

Camouflaging ferns at sea
offer places to reside
for little fish that otherwise
would be a snack on any tide

Inland from the sea a brake
of ferns house woven nests
of thrushes that would certainly be
served up to a cat's request

But whether lodging fins or wings
both were made for hiding things

Dress Rehearsal

Beyond two lakes near Logan's Pass
stand dawn like calloused pines
gale-carved cliffs on up the timber
muted recording time

Caretaking earth recalls each leaf
in North Valley far below
the gentle colors merging, then
failing I watch them go

Golden strands of ageless sunlight
eclipsing through the trees
bronze and yellow rays displacing
the falling autumn leaves

Muffled in thin, distant vapor
ringing across King's Bay
honkings, cryings, migrants flying
south to Flamingo Cay

Amid this windswept, open glade
wind dancing with elfin nods
one remaining mountain laurel
waving goodbye to God.

Scarlet oak and Christmas holly
engage this broken way
tender forgotten memories
hailing from yesterday

Closing skies of crimson splendor
casting resplendent hues
drifting clouds enflame at sunset
sail beneath majestic blues

Sleep filled the night here descending
claiming all things alow
soon tapping soft, sole invited
silver impressive snow

Twisting wreaths of ice are forming
clinging methodically

to woodland arbors canopied
with crystal, snow-bowed trees

A wintry, half-moon, amber light
defines the sleeping timber
sterling, star-glazed, haunting sights
this time of year is hard to render

Dawn

How strange, yet beautiful is night
infused with advancing light
occluding swift our view afar
the silent distant Venus star

Describing now each flower face
of long awaited Queen Anne's lace
and gossamer designed in dew
night so carefully hid from view

Boob Tube

In the course of daily chores
I sat for a coffee break
decided to watch the morning news
to see what was at stake

The remote control did not work
the TV was a blank
probably batteries I thought out loud
old and pass'd their rank

I searched the house thoroughly twice
one new one's all I found
Put it in with one of the old
to check it out for sound

I settled down and turned it on
Like any amateur
with one old battery and one new, I
only got half a picture

Change You Can Bank On

Like the winging of a sparrow
or the swiftness of an arrow
hence the passing of the hours
I sense the change of thundershowers

Everything in switching motion
the rising, falling tidal ocean
friction adjusting in a bower
I sense the changing of closing flowers

What was today won't be tomorrow
mirth can even shift to sorrow
I come with thought of this pre-notion
I sense a way to stop all motion

Reversing the way of all rotation
stemming the double graduation
but then I thought beyond today
It'd still be change any way

Exit the Garden

Gone the dateless worlds of fragmenting stars
when instinct ruled an age of errant ways
the sum of human suffering slack of hope
was in a brief encounter brought to bay

Invisible by dreams, abject refugees
were showered with the gift of reasoning
when God gave man a trusting partnership
reason woke the soul and set it on the wing

The birth of soul gave life a different course
no more the hidden order of the dead
the grace of reason bid the awakened soul
eternal life for unborn tomorrows instead

The will and testament of this public gift
a book of instructions to run from day to day
emerging from the paradisiac garden side
looking for the eternal entrance way

As doors locked out the pilot dust of man
the dawn of reckoning will graft from me
a fateful drama of a self in beaten robes
that one will be the master of the key

Having taken man from hapless strife
in its place the seeds of hope were sown
the writing on this page will end now
since here each man can make it on his own

Screws 'n Bolts

I had a job in a nut factory
working from twelve to nine
if you were late you went home early
to make up for lost time

The Wish

That I would be like warm, worn
furniture wearing well
comfortably aging
with oaken smells
valued not for trade
precious, not for sale

Betti's Boutique
(dolls and things)

If the puppets were to speak
in silence as they stare
at walls arrowed
with cross-stitched kin
some in tux, some in tatter
Raggedy Ann and scarecrows
eager, ready to go
perhaps the prom, perhaps the show
the bridal pair touching hands
on her finger his wedding band
lovely, alert to go
out the door to a lovers' abode
disturbing the warm, rustic air
came the sound of shoppers' chatter
haggling over the bride,
the groom was silly matter
then her had wrapped from head to toe
thinking a cute, collectible thing
leaving the groom in the dusty room
holding tight their wedding ring

Placcs for Things

How could there be more lovely
than wild daisies afield
year upon year they remember
after winter to yield

In show they go far ranging
yellow in bloom they flow
stretching beyond fair reason
across the valley they go

Then up a hill to where a place
in line but not arow
the daisies stop then start back down
to let some scrub pines grow

Photographs

Comparing her graceful shape of ten plus six
to when she was a toothless girl, not chic
from the album one by one she drew the pics
and let them drop by one into a mix
of daily sweepings from the floor

Mom, a witness to this act of desecration
sorely thinking in her meditation
one discarding things into a heap
another one would dearly, gladly keep

On the Boardwalk

Somewhere among the crowd, lovers
touching, signaling unheard
understanding and committing
without the use of words

Undoubting, feeling, expressing
in a language much its own
Lovers lost in the noise of a crowd
conversing with eyes alone

The White Dwarf

Transporting the white hot energy
into a spiraling galactic hole
from a speckled quadrant of drowning stars
leaving just one for a different role

Compacting, squeezing cosmic forces
create a living something narrow
the magnetic bang of the universe
fashions a seat of ultimate power

(the petals of an unfolding age shape and densify
a bubble into a practicing new world)

Magnetizing, luring disordered debris
and overflowing ruin from distant yield
racing through distorted time and space
to blanket an atomized nuclear field

Infusing scores of infinite matter
enlarge the growing infant mass
green intelligence assembles the bowl
as time stands still, while eons pass

Flaring particles from captured stars
impact the tight developing skin
persuasive rhythm nudges the earth
into an orbital elliptical spin

Hallowed ground in titanic convulsions
splitting the land mass apart
molding, shaping, landscaping our world
directed from the inner heart

Age by age the sea trickles in
controlling the seismic atmosphere
volcanic action beneath the sea
reaches the upper stratosphere

Rising heat and trailing vapors
star in the solitude of light
composing wind, spiraling sailing
across the sea to find the night

Strokes of starlight pattern eddies
as rippling ether curves and planes
spiraling convexing vapors admixins
building clouds to bring the rains

Outstretched and fallow the naked earth
mixes the seeds of yon present star
with dust and rain create beginnings
of life donated from miles afar

Forces within the belly of earth
arrange the planet's wavered steering
and command other roles from pole to pole
courtesy of celestial engineering

Untitled Sleep

Night, when all men are equal
vulnerable only to dreams
common, incomprehensible
patterns rise and fall
across each inner screen
stripped of names and titles
just phantoms in a dream
alone in the arms of Morpheus
alone on the silent screen
waking to breaking sunlight
that makes a prism of dew
bowing before an August king
begins again anew

A Dream in Purgatory

In these secluded chambers
private and absent of soul
shut against this inward sorrow
she enlisted in secret approach

(I did not hear her come
I did not hear her go)

Silent in mystic entry
forthright in arcane entry
against impregnable entry
she handed a single rose

(I did not hear her come
nor did I hear her go)

In those stout-walled chambers
sworn against access
where alone I bear this sorrow
she handed a covert rose

(I would not hear her come
I would not hear her go)

Hidden from every entry
alone retired to woe
a single, red, orphic rose
returned my missing soul

(I'm fain to hear her come
I'm fain not hear her go)

In these sheltered enclosures
relieved now from this pain
an Angel of covert mystery
rewrote my missing name

(in dream I saw her come
in dream I glimpsed her go)

An Inverted View

The knock was heavy upon the plate
a note one risk not ignore
whoever was doing the rapping
so needing in this door

I rose in doubt and went to see
straightforward to deplore
who was sent in graven tapping
desiring entry into my door

Reluctantly I turned the key
then stepped aback to see
a silver crowned, Athenian face
fair looking down at me

She came inside with courtly grace
a vision to explore
then brushed stellar dust from her hair
that gleamed upon the floor

I've come this way in midnight flight
that brings me to your door
in lieu of one, Apollo, she said
and woo help to restore

The glory that once pervaded Greece
beauty that gods adore
assist me in this grief tonight
with mystical verse of yore

These texts I quote are truly wise
no worship for caprice
and cannot light your way without
your journey ends in peace

But let your quest not end so brief
these scripts intone of truth
when grief was healed with compassion
surely the shadow of Ruth

She turned each page, each numbered book
each line while did devour

The Never Ending Cosmic Show

without a pause, without a rest
far pass this urgent hour

She rose at last unconfounded
voicing a different view
little sorrow had turned to grace
trusting these scriptures too

Blue Eyes Came Back for Me

I fooled one eye in nodding dreaming
and held in reverie
impressions I found beseeming
blue eyes of destiny

By her leave we tripped in flying
awash in harmony
fancy in going hand in hand
down lanes of memory

She paused along the country road
I thought to reminisce
Instead she pulled me down to grass
and sealed my lips in kiss

I've never met a fate like this
this old life now I shun
not giving a damn what she is
blue eyed huzzy or a nun

A Christmas Tree Is...

Brown, soft eyes within the tree
blinking, looking up at me
perched somewhat above the snow
a little thrush I did not know

So small a thing in this vast land
if sat upon an open hand
would not shade a lot of skin
no bigger than the smallest wren

Trembling before the silent cold
his tiny breast not thrust out bold
as apprehension began to grow
for surely my intent he did not know

Closing the limbs I did divide
to seal the warmth that was inside
I sheathed the ax and turned around
then from the hillside went back down

Thinking on saying to Emily
let's bu some facsimile
mumbling to God absently
no way in hell I'll chop that tree

Juice From These Grapes

Caked was the floor in the bar room
from stools back to the door
with sawdust reeking of lager
here in the saloon Red Boar

In from the night did he enter
in through the swinging door
across the ale room unsteady
approaching me to explore

I bore into his countenance
as he came upon me nigh
the gods never warned me of these
haunting indentured eyes

Some wine, he said, I'm needing
to calm this midnight chill
a pint of Port would ally me
I beg you if you will

He drank `til the jug was empty
then flush came to his face
the hands were now more steady
and straight lined was his pace

His thanks was real and lingering
and said, I don't want more
I'm going to sleep in that field tonight
then rose to go for the door

I'm fine tonight but morning I'll wake
and need more than a toddy
for each grasshopper that hops the grass
will sound like somebody

Relatives

My uncle was a reasonable
suspect for failure
first he tried stealing chickens
and ran afowl of the law
when he got out of jail
he tried crossing
a chicken with an owl
and came up with a foul owl
so then he tried to breed
the howlet out of the fowl
and came up with a
little hooter that clucked
he took the little clucking hooter
to a county fair and wond
first prize in an oddity show
radio station W.H.O. was airing
the event when a bird fancier
named I.M. Duper heard about
the tiny clacking whooper
profit in an inkling
crossed his line of thinking

My uncle O.I. Hirtz was so proud of
that little crackling, scratching hooter
that he wouldn't sell his bird
to I.M. Duper
undaunted Dupe talked him into
an exhibition woe
called the H. & D. Curio Show
the lone revue toured
from town to city to town
wherever carnivals abound
with under light success
so they decided to invest
in something as a booster
they drove to a Bantam chicken farm
went in with larceny in mind
forgot to lock the show cage from behind
the owl snuck out and ran off with the rooster

There's Poetry in Everything
(All You Need Is a Rhyming Scheme)

The bat was eying the cat
sneaking upon the rat
while she chewed the farmers hat
oh gee, by golly, that's where it's at

Linkage

When the claiming crashing sea
reaches out and frightens me
I turn and go another way
inland to a flattened bay
there becalmed but then heartsore
I trek back to the active shore
for seas and me are of the same
accounting meaning more than name
as I have learnt the truthful score
from evidence the latest lore
that long ago from out the sea
a shape arose the start of me
Tho temperamental she may be
and doesn't look alike to me
sea, sea though motherless be
by your wit created me

Act IV
The Judgment

In gold, rich judicial chambers
where Caesar's bust thrones the door
the trial of proof began to untangle
when prosecution took the floor

Impersonating a King the charge
levied against the shackled man
performing miracles the second crime
unlicensed by an Emperor's ban

Exalted priests launched their case
only Rome can parent a king
this imposter falsely professes
the title of "King of Kings"

A round of witnesses testified
he never solicited a fee
for miracles performed in numbers
all the productions were free

His plea to heavenly wonders
and Lord of all the Kings
can you believe this delivery
when he has no crown or ring?

The closing argument ere the verdict
came down like a curtain call
this fabricating, illusioned actor
doesn't wear crested jewelry at all

Act V
The Crucifixion
(To Fetch a Trophy)

Enterprisingly still and quiet
earth's entry into morn
with antlered silhouettes transfixed
to see this dawn be born

Ere before the collapsing night
began to wane and thin
pride awakened from weak slumber
the hunters for spoil again

Now with long, terrifying leaps
the deer break on a run
as wanton shot confounds the glade
`twixt sleep and the rising sun

Crimson struck inanimate kneed
buck and horns go down in stride
frightened, confused, and bewildered
the doe looks back wide-eyed

Broken, sightless so hushed in death
once soft and harmless eyed
the bell has rung the day is on
where one gentle thing had died

Close Encounters

The silent opening of morning glories
the fertile action of fumbling bees
prisms of light where grass meets dew
enchanted woods to wander through
a wave of wheat across the plain
the welcome sound of falling rain
the smell of newly mown hay
the scent of seaweed off the bay
the wind pushing the sea outside
the moon pulling in the tide
the perfect order of stars in time
a poem in balanced metric rhyme
and would there be other roads
to profit on these thoughts
I'd seek them as the winter searched
to find the spring it brought

The Debut

Peace, an alien so rare on stage
reading script from an empty page
unwritten leaves except one place
approaching hell is the human race

Rituals

Shades of night come softly calling
on the umbered river falling
naught the light does fain protest
the world into the night invests

Against the sky shapes are forming
to silhouettes thus transforming
this the shaping of the trees
round and tall in twos and threes

Shadows now the moon in casting
luminescent stars are massing
dust is left to dew's command
twilight stirs the dream demand

Bush along the moonlit river
struck in hues of ambered silver
quick the chicks are eased to sleep
in nests: warm, dry, nestled deep

The wind, now curious, searches clover
for aroma sealed as buds close over
day cares flight, a swift retreat
the night rules now sleep, sleep, sleep

Starred and still the earth revealing
a finite glance fleet receding
allowing in this August night
a glimpse of God in this half light

Uncle Sam

Go to work from nine `til five
can the drinking when you drive
don't walk against a warning light
go not alone in the night

Eat bran for breakfast every day
oh, do relax and do some play
be in bed by ten o'clock
don't forget the deadbolt lock

See your doctor once a year
keep the pool clean for your ear
floss your teeth every week
stay off the freeway at its peak

Save some money at the bank
wear galoshes when it's dank
watch your weight and don't get fat
in the sun put on a hat

With all these things I'm told to do
by governments, the likes of you
I'll never think of death nor why
they'll let me know when to die

The New Chimney

A bad winter we had of it
snow trapped among these hills
wisely using what fuel there was
to fend the nightly chills

Then spring arrived just soon enough
and eased the cold away
but spring can't ease these memories
of the bitter winter days

There's a lot of trees I said
to chop for heating wood
let's deal to have a fireplace built
topped with a snow sloped hood

The plans were drawn; the contract signed
they started right away
I watched each step, brick by brick
a little strange their way

Never we thought ever was seen
such handsome work before
the freezing fears as winter nears
are with us now no more

The fire was lit as frost set in
yule logs were in the bin
the stack wouldn't let black smoke out
only fresh cold air in

I phoned the builder pleading loudly
we need help right away
a tape replied: closed for winter
see you again in May

Truant

Be not unkind, April, that I
don't browse the fields in search
of your adulterous fling and sight
the first leaves on the birch

But finds me beached between the tide
a little less for raw
the winter snows were much too deep
I need some time to thaw

Making Blue

Lean on the wind, trumpet player
push on sad notes; round `em off
moan like the wind on a lonely night
wail like the sobs of a broken heart
keep it lean; mute the sounds
making the blues coming `round

Lean on the wind, trumpet player
divide the night with hungry sighs
cry like souls lost in flight
trombones sliding, saxes oozing down
easing the blues coming `round

Lean on the wind, O' jazz man
blow the blue notes: round `em off
make `em weep go: go get down
making the blues coming `round

Lean on the wind...

The Spring of Gardens and War

Beauty awaits the arriving admirers
where charm exists in tranquil bowers

(Ministers of arms with phantom fleets
pledging victory to fervid beats)

Quietly lilacs sprout coffined rows
obeying sunlight their path to grow

(war drums throbbing, ensigns flying
man made hell comes and the dying)

Bees earn nectar for honeycombs
an income from roses and blossoms unknown

(destruction abounds while cannons roar
fears of defeat haunt vanity's door)

Patient spiders weave trapping lairs
thistle spores winging on steering air

(war's quick fire blights all in sight
armies obsessed in all out flight)

Sunflowers practice their faith on high
following their God across the sky

(the tragic note about war's vain glories
giving man medals for what he destroys)

Where Goes the Heart

We soar on the wings of love
we rise to untamed episodes
we fly in the face of danger
we run where fools wouldn't go
we climb the ladder of success
we reach beyond the distant shores
we journey afar; in separate ego
the human soul
looks back at gathering clouds
seeking God untiringly
over conscious, elipsing earth
knowing time will bring us down

Time and the Sea

And the sea was a long time in coming
hidden by pristine cosmic dust
yet light from a comforting star
urged life forms to rise and adjust

And somewhere twixt the sun and moon
alone in the vast global swirl
the sea from plants spawned breath
and main life began to unfurl

And the beauty unleashed from the ocean
took root on the desolate shore
erelong the sky covered forests
luring birds and fauna to explore

And the ancestry of lovely trees
blueprinted the building of man
bonding complex cells together
guided skillfully by the draftman's hand

And this union, this prolific wedding
between an ocean and a visiting star
rained echoes down from the universe
of applause however afar

And the land became a haven
for all creatures grand and small
the music of life drafting history
on a planet for one and all

And innate fleetings of changing tides
distant memories that served him yore
man was drawn back to the sea
and early footprints upon the shore

And the sea becalmed as he drew near
an invitation to well explore
man was born with faithful wonder
pondering life once here before

And pioneering in the pacific waters
then rising up through the rippling foam

the first Baptist had just one witness
the thundering rider who called him home

In Preparation of Man

In one titanic primeval explosion
ignited by the draftsman's hand
without dimensions aeons ago
the epic cosmic passage began

Thundering, expanding pursuing no end
an elegant process in it's prime
creating opportunistic gravity
the moving fabric of space and time

Spiral galaxies, pinwheels of dust
began in the macrocosm of space
thermonuclear reactions launched
the birth of starts to guide this place

In a spiral arm the Earth was born
exquisite example of cosmic design
with Gamma, X and Radio waves
when the Sun plunged through Orion

Fifteen billion years unfolding
surviving endless catastrophes
welcome now to the planet Earth
of green meadows and abundant seas

A world rippling with myriad life
journeying through time, live and aware
human beings born of the stars
strikingly beautiful and ever so rare

The surface of Earth became a shore
to look out and see the cosmic plan
surrounded by velvet galactic space
where the birth and song of man began

Lost somewhere in a timeless vacuum
tucked inside a galactic swirl
randomly carved into the cosmos
a floating dot we call our world

Alone in the universal court
of intergalactic permanent night

stars pinpoint the way to forever
faintly flickering in guiding light

Fragmenting to ashes and infinite dust
stellar matter aneath compression
by supernova shocking waves
breeding a new star formation

The new stars roam afar from home
as offspring frequently do
seeking their fortune on the Milky Way
like children, suns have parents too

Nature's Nickelodeon

The solo of the Oriole
is number one on the chart
a mortal bird with colored words
waging illicit war on a heart

The lonesome trill of a whipoorwill
at dusk from where I stood
enhancing the kindest hour of day
coming from deep inside yon wood

Yellow breasted, low in flight
a mournful whistling Meadowlark
signals the closing of summer's day
repairing her nest before it's dark

Soft caroling of Golden Sparrows
giving a wistful soul a start
winging down this country road
pulling psyche a bit apart

Standing before a splintered sky
hearing enchanting chords and keys
shorn of pride, sprinkled with grace
recording Arias such as these

The First Edition

And creation started so suddenly
terminable and gladsome was the sound
and the cosmos went sprawling undying
birthing galaxies were swift to abound

The reeling question if unrestrained
when the universe of stars began
would the genesis of planets endanger
the splendid race of coming man

Confronted with nebula out of control
the riddle furrowed the mind of God
a section of infinity robbed of space
by matter mathematically odd

Tearing a piece out of the universe
in each and every galaxy
moderating this widening taste
would rein the growth of infinity

Controlling the rivers of gas and dust
the road to where clusters are born
creating secular employment
by inserting a black hole form

Gravity unleashed through cosmic holes
pulling against the leagues of space
collecting fragments of bursting stars
balancing growth by passionate grace

Compacting, compressing, squeezing matter
into the minutest of form
storing debris, keeping the heavens free
of reusable parts is part of the norm

When the rising need as galaxies recede
and spaces are sole behind
the black holes explode. Recycling starstuff
forming new worlds, much like their kind

The Canopy

Pale blue scented Ozone gases
covering the Earth's outer field
when the sun's ultraviolet light
splits oxygen forming a protective shield

Guarding something beautiful as Earth
filled with snowflakes and fireflies
shrouding the long journey of man
from conception until he dies

Every stage of nature reveals
birth and dependence on our star
but what good is sun radiation
if not filtered to Earth from afar

Powered by sifted cosmic light
trees are redeemable collectors
trading carbon gas for oxygen
converted from their leafy pores

Traffic throughout the universe
destined to visit eternally
comets bring from different worlds
new voices of life exclusively

The habitability of Earth
and the destiny of man
evolves around a thin blue haze
constructed with a secret plan

Our obligation to survive
and participate under ozone
man must stop turning this cover
into a contaminating war zone

(war is a childhood sickness
no doctor has found a cure for
the reptilian part of man's cortex
lies undeveloped in the core)

In Search Of

Sunlight plunging through galactic planes
targeting blue planet earth
an elegant process of cosmic creation
the first stage of every birth

The comfort of superstition is bypassed
creation of life is by light alone
the uniqueness of flesh here manifested
on a beautiful world we call our home

Born of the stars, inquisitively seeking
other planets such as our own
hoping to find equal inhabitants
a solace to know we are not alone

The Fifth Dimension

Time, the invisible breadth where in we compete
from birth through youth and maturity
ever aspiring until we champion no more
rafting the river of change, flowing outward bound
like a dying star collapsing, plunging
through a cosmic hole in the space time continuum
vanishing from the universe for eternity
these parallel dimensions allow the soul
in it's journey to come back home to God

Celestial Engineering

In the thundering spiraling beginning
from unrich shadows came atomic light
stars began emerging flickering
along the corridors of crumbling night

The astral architect posed one question
weighing no matter left behind
why the cosmos had no substance
"was starless night flying blind?"

Anon the suns received instructions
curve and plane the universe
unlock the planet's heroic soils
rid this dark and senseless curse

Thinner than thread with careful fingers
sink seep your rays into the earth
pull back the pall of anemic night
activate and give it birth

Plough the sea with flaming light
north and south to give it life
crowd the system, design a man
publish history engineer a wife

Warm the planets, lift up clouds
until they hail with lovely rain
nourish trees with life giving leaves
sprout the fields with survival grain

Stars, all mothers by distant birth
of every pulse and future kin
comets and asteroids circle the worlds
bearing gifts on the solar wind

Man quickly grew inventing science
probing learning with vainful minds
avowing per logic establishing facts
owing himself all celestial finds

He scientifically proved without a doubt
the universe began with a burst

adulating, but neglecting to note
that this kingdom, had existed first

Forecast Earth

The utilities of the universe are stars
keeping the cosmos up and running
generating sunlight, animating earth
stellar realty gave us conception
cosmic productions are endless and assuring
a breath taking view of evolving worlds

One can savor with sheer delight
the early sanction of their creation
electrical forces between atoms is the
gravitational language of the stars
while some move with gentle grace
others go careening through infinite space

We are made of intergalactic starstuff
man and trees are akin in ancestral function
both breathing in and breathing out
humans are more alike than they are diverse
yet our resources are dwindling; fighting wars
while mutating the genetic code of life

One day the sun will be a phantom of itself
dying in the birth of it's only child
the fate of the inner solar system will be grim
starlight on this outpost Earth is our future
our origin is the sum of cosmic engineering
it is time we find and begin our journey home

Genesis
(The Architect)

With the creation of man, God spent his search
for a witness to memorize and record
the journey and symphonic beauty of the universe

The journal having been passed, reads from page to page
of a primal cosmos where things change, not by chance
but according to celestial engineering laws

Where interplanetary gravity, born of light
parents harmony between planets and moons
a musical equation throughout eternity

Our world, tracking a thermonuclear sun
conforming to the rules of planetary motion
gluing man from Genesis, to the face of the earth

Enveiling our shores in orderly grace
a mystic shielding shroud, of connate blue
leasing life systems like the human race

Majestic galaxies of planets and stars
are the beautiful productions of nature
drifting forever through intergalactic night

The stars are assuring, flickering eternal
the exploration of the universe is endless
seeking ourselves, we are children of astral dust

Every star system is an island in space
flooding the cosmos with life breeding light
for planetary surfaces to harbor new life

We harvest sunlight, our planet is solar powered
the stars lend us worth to make us whole
the inventory of life is enormous

Our future lies in a distant star, when our sun
explodes, becoming a specter of itself, then
from the ashes, give birth to it's only child

Our journey to the stars is a difficult one

beset by playing war games with our destiny
while peaces lies undiscovered before us

The stars pulsate the the rhythmic throbbing waves
glittering, spinning, twirling, keeping time
moving like ballet dancers, on the milky way

These orchestrated cosmic arrangements
of stellar properties, on loan to me and you
move a silent heart, inawed with the view

(and somewhere in this timeless space
set inside a spiral swirl
is a vested rock, we call our world)

Carving out the Earth

Traveling light years thru twilight space
a fiery part of an exploding star
passed thru the east of Taurus
on through Orion then much afar

Coming at last to a tentacle wisp
in the galaxy Milky Way
positioning by gravity
the shell of Earth was now to stay

Collecting debris thru eons of time
til Earth in size did expand
volcanic heat pushing upwards
changed the character of the land

Graven mountains on display
rose above a desolate land
solar winds molding stone and clay
as if guided by a sculptor's hand

As landmasses heightened in numbers
basins were carved out below
the greatest mystery then began
where from did the water flow

Vaporous heat from the remnant star
eructing rising in the cosmic air
amending hydrogen to hydrous liquid
the sea was born by this precious pair

A new star formed east of Taurus
steered by gravity's control
plunged thru the Orion constellation
arriving hear Earth was it's goal

Lifeless, infertile was the planet
when the new star acted as host
pouring ultraviolet radiation
the sun turned life on from it's post

(when stars are spent collapse and die
from the ashes is born, it's only child)

The War on Peace

Peace the sister of sweet tolerance
suffering, banned from the human race
where patient fruits lie unripened
a harvest lost of gentle grace

War an act ill classified
like wise counsel gone astray
like main springs broken in the mind
like thunder on a silent cloudless day

The precious children of our world
parenterally trapped in a poison bud
learning curious superstitions
might breeds right from spilling blood

Until this venom is traced to the bulb
uprooted hacked til the vine is slain
this harvest of dear innocent puppets
will teach their sons the same refrain

Sunrise, bent on errands of the day
creating life in the sea and land
intently drafting wind and rain
unrattled by warring views of man

Rainbows

Somewhere I have never seen rain
fall so carefully
as if from some great distance
to the ground
there was ever enough time
slowly, gently, silently
to find the way down
bending across the noon day
summer, mist, touching
Earth without sound
an arch of red, yellow and blue
describing where to me and you
the gift of rain was passing thru

The A B C's of Earth

"A"

The great Alaskan ice-shelf
in all its majestic grace
blue and sterling reflections
gleaming from it's crystal face

The morning sun suggesting
from the frozen beauty arrayed
silently entombed in time
cosmic planning here displayed

The fountain of glacial streams
in stock for a change of clime
a reservoir of frozen assets
preserved for a warmer time

"B"

Titans of massive forest
stretching Brazilian land
refining carbon impurities
supporting the life of man

Laboring sifting environmentally
the weave and fabric of trees
producing precious oxygen
from lovely extending leaves

The dignity of Mother Earth
from warring man to worker bee
hangs precariously with out reins
the dwindling forests hold the key

"C"

Beyond the deserts in China's mountains
huddling together, complex machines
harvesting converting sunlight
allotting spaces for vital streams

Though different in shapes and sizes

ancestral roots link man and trees
wailing is heard when children die
with trees it's a mourning breeze

The Gobi is dry where fossils lie
over a dusty and barren plain
the absence of trees and magic leaves
remind us the urgent need of rain

"E"

England, where the Gulf stream flows
favoring the island with temperate clime
the sea carving prehistoric shores
the moving fabric of space and time

The present beauty of rolling hills
meadows alive with stock and ties
pasture feeding and the rain relying on
lighting recharging nitrogen skies

Skilled on existence the island nation
recycling water to stay alive
enriching rain feeding the grass
carrying nitrogen from wide blue skies

"F"

The Lascaux caves in Durdogne Valley
ages ago in southwest France
neanderthals dependent on the hunt
with primitive ax and wooden lance

In the Ardennes and other forests
animals are killed just for sport
ungracious guests in witless quest
drawn from inns and tourist resort

Eagles nesting yon rugged cliffs
witness the early stages of death
the faltering fauna in final throes
drawing a little dying breath

"G"

Greek philosophers reached the shores
of the mystifying cosmic ocean
unable to define stars and lightening
made Gods of any alien notion

Ionian influence of Grecian culture
revealed wind wasn't the breath of God
and stars were not stellar candles
lighting the way for man to trod

Randomly exploring ancient fables
what can't be explained must be divine
remanding their Gods to the sole clockmaker
setting Earth's cycles in perfect time

"H"

Pulsating inside Earth's shifting shell
a White Dwarf's hot degenerate mass
pushing massive matter upward
and volcanoes spewing stellar gas

Slowly the many Hawaiian islands
began their arduous journey through Earth
a dynamic force beyond comprehension
bearing sea girt land by cosmic birth

Anon the cooling shores bore flowers
and trees damp with propagating dew
tropical panorama gripped the islands
giving nested birds, a pageantary view

"I"

Israel the cradle of salvation
all that will be happened here
the souls lonely roaming after death
ended with a death and grieving tear

In distant memories men speculate
creating religious isms by the score
interpretations dicing with truth
of happenings where in the days of yore

This tiding didn't cause disputed views
man's ego bred religious wars before
the star of this production cared only
to open up salvation's keyless door

"J"

Jurassic a time for careful creation
trees arriving charging space on high
with oxygen pioneering a basic climate
colonizing the land sea and sky

With birds, fish, flowers and maiden things
emerging from the depths of a living sea
gently dinosaurs tiptoed out in their prime
leaving only their footsteps and bone debris

Grand mountains covered with breathing forest
valleys and streams shaped by nature's hand
this planet was built for worlds to see
and celebrate the coming of cosmic man

"K"

Kuwait a harsh ground of desert winds
misleading rain clouds astray
funneling western thermal breezes
scattering the laden nimbus way

Catalog the question of survival
what must be done to dwell here
desalinate the Gulf's wealthy waters
and pray clouds shed an ample tear

Orphaned and alone of needed rain
severity another blow delivers
where thin precious showers fall
on a land without any rivers.

Attending the Air Show

Morning broke and I awoke
facing a pale Denver sky
`till the clouds were fused with sunlight
cycloraming for the awakened eye

The pious planning of a star
lifting vapors over the earth
then painting the mist with color
giving the sky panoramic birth

North, East, West, and South engraving
under a fragile canopy
the wind carves likened images
of things on Earth we often see

As the north winds roll and rise
an outline comes into view
of mountain ranges expansing
tinted purple, white and blue

Then to the east above the woods
rising high a mystic tower
beneath it's walls on little feet
dance ghostly swaying flowers

Westerly winds swirling shaping
a flattened shark without a fin
and the front of an elephant
ears and trunk but missing his end

A southern caravan of clouds
reveal a desert ship as sea
and when the scudding haze treks clear
I see the edge of eternity

Knowing not the day nor hour
this world I look upon in light
is full of wonder but the fate
of these delights belong to night

Brown Sugar and Green Tea
(things we commonly see)

Red strawberries and green peas
giant redwood and mahogany trees

Gray and great blue herons
indigo and painted buntings
red and white blooms on a twig

Orange carrots and purple grapes
carmine beets and velvet drapes

Olive and orange crowned warblers
ruby and gold topped kinglets
violet and freckled butterflies

Pink hibiscus and crimson roses
mauve lilacs and clown red noses

Green and black hooded parrots
scarlet and white faced ibis
silver moon risings and golden sunsets

Lemon citrus and honey pot ants
yellow squash and blond eggplant

The yellow river and coral sea
autumn valleys and snowy hills
red, white, black and amber children

From Earth to the edge of eternity
without the stars, there's nothing to see.

The Refinery

Owing my lifeway to a tree
launching oxygen I can breathe
cool and beautiful to one's eye
without trees I would surely die

Springtime is time for leaf openings
watch how the foliage dearly clings
so the nude glade can be shaded
by boughs from sunlight created

Summer is the time, the season
when trees show the world good reason
snorting carbon dust through the leaves
cleansing man made dirt as it breathes

Autumn is time for color displays
leaves announce an end of their days
graphically falling one by one
obeying an order from the sun

Winter buries beneath the snow
foliage where bare branches show
and flowers that in the springtime grow
nourishing roots that sleep below

Loggers reaped where once was shade
logging oaks breathing from the glade
then from the mill packaged so neat
came products of oaken toilet seats

Celestial Engineering

The Gift

Created by the sun, born into a world of
authored light, surrounded by intricate
cosmic wonders, man embarked upon a
timeless bond with creation healing the
terrible hunger of solitude witnessed
by God.
The order now complete, each species
developed it's own attraction.
The activity of the sun is endless, we
are solar powered.
Life on Earth runs on sunlight.
Ultra violet radiation pours into Earth's
atmosphere, generating lightning and thunder
thunder, like shaking deep baritone voices
that meant to sing.
The sun warms and feeds us, it is powerful
far beyond human experience.
Farming is the methodical harvesting of
it's light.
Animals absorb the chemical energy of plants.
Birds greet the sunrise with chirping ecstasy,
while one celled organisms know to swim to
the light.
And far from the shore at sunset
across the silent sea
beautiful sky impressions
that did not belong to me
and everywhere the universe
endlessly sweeping disclosing
the luminary range of God and
sounds of infinity unfolding

Keep the Changes Flowing

Global peace is a kind of arrogant
new comer to Earth, after thousands
of years of war and aggression
Humans everywhere share the same goal,
bury war or write a prescription
for disaster.
For the first time in history, major
moronic wars are losing their appeal.
Sweeping global rational changes are
moving in the proper directions
needed for our survival.
All our past accomplishments are not
but the awakening from a dream,
in our littleness believing that
might is right.
We are living in a tiny fragile world
lost in the immensity of eternity and
have held the peculiar notion that
persons and societies that are different
from us should be distrusted and
despised.
But yet we have compassion for others
and love for our children, the tools
we need for continued survival.
Our task now, is to recognize that we
are all one species living on this
tiny delicate world where our obligation,
"less we forget" is owed to that ancient
divine beginning from whence we all came

Gambling With Earth

In the beginning ash from dying stars created
a small sphere of stone and iron, this was the
dawn of our world.
Then raindrops of hot interstellar dust forged
Earth, atom by atom level by level.
When the planet had cooled, it released water
and gasses to create a primitive atmospheric
blanket, this ozonic cover so light, so blue,
allowing sunlight passage through was interwoven
with delicate threads of care and grace the
blueprint of a home for the coming of man.
And now somewhere in eternity our tiny land
floats like a speck of dust in this immeasurable
universe.
Welcome to the cosmos, after millions of years
under construction, today beautiful and
uncommonly rare.
We are gifted with a universe where life is
sparked by sunlight and every aspect of nature
reveals a great mystery.
There are many other worlds where life has
never arisen
Through the cosmic hydrogen industry of atoms
all life on Earth is microscopically related
and yet instead of admitting that the differences
between humans and their views is
trivial compared to their similarities, we
have chosen war to settle these differences.
Four million years ago there were no humans
now dangerous adolescence can cancel who
will be here the next million years
A full nuclear exchange would burn the oxygen
in the upper ozone converting it to oxides
allowing ultra violet radiation from the sun
to produce cancer and to destroy crops,
this, this would end civilization as we know
it, a confession finally to the stupidity
of war

Dawn of The Cosmos

It has taken twenty billion free years to develop
from timeless space our universe and the last four
and a half billion to construct an inviting
versatile, beautiful home for the coming of man.
Slowly, carefully from molten iron and nickel to the
outer earthen crust, planet earth was built without
a schedule.
Engineered and methodically assembled out of nuclear
fusioned fragments and dust, from aging, dying, exploding
stars. And as this world neared completion, weaving
through the galaxy Orion a single star came to rest
near Earth to breed all life on the planet
This, this was the beginning of the universe, time
without dimensions, an everlasting night of intergalactic
distance.
Warming, solidifying, Earth released methane, water,
and hydrogen gasses to form it's primitive protective
atmosphere and now far above the land, amassing white
clouds fluffed by angelic winds adorn the beautiful
azure skies, yearning to behold the first citizen
of the universe, Earth, a master stage from where he
can explore and treasure this infinite cosmic ocean
of light, awakening a kindred view to set sail
homeward, for the talented stars

The Never Ending Cosmic Show

In the great infinite darkness, stars in a
continuous celebration of
creation spread life across time and space.
The smoldering wonder of nuclear fusion
forging all the elements needed for new
worlds make this cosmic architecture a
thing of miraculous beauty.
The excess of galaxies has a story to
tell us of beginning events on the largest
possible scale,
In this universal picture the birth of a star
from an erupting parent star produces the
loveliest field of color set against the
velvet of intergalactic space.
The stars of the Milky Way move with an
orderly grace, as groups plunge through
the galactic plane to the other side
then reverse and hurdle back again.
Not far outside the galaxy there are other
planets orbiting stars that surround the
Milky Way, such worlds would offer a breathtaking
view of the universe in endless motion.
The size of the cosmos is beyond human
understanding, we only know that this
is the greatest of mysteries.
There is an order, a predictability
about the stars, one can make a superior
calendar of their comings and goings.
The origin of life is connected to the origin
of stars in the most intimate way, the
calcium in our teeth and the iron in our blood
were made in the fusion of stars, we are
made of starstuff.
Finally at the end of our travels through space
we return to our tiny world, welcome to
planet Earth.
The grandeur and intricacy of nature set
before me, blue breathable skies, oceans
of fluid water, shading forests, and gentle
meadows, in the cosmic perspective is
beautiful and rare and for a moment unique.
Standing, completely absorbed in this elaborate

creation, when suddenly I felt as if someone
had gently touched my hand

A Copy Of

Precious earth your space in time
curious man of ancient wonder
habitating this island land
a marvel to audit and to wonder

Not counting the ages while creating
industrious fingers of delight
organizing man from stardust
fathering along the cosmic night

Weaving together the bones of man
careful not to brand the skin
when the task was finally over
behold a mixture of related kin

A sense of bright awakening
met man's first observing eyes
glimpsing an inkling of infinity
while looking his fill into the skies

The beauty of the universe
utopic to the human mind
the blueprints secretly classified
an enigma for all mankind

In this stout and bossy clime
the vicious work of Satan loomed
assassinating sacred airs
condemning purity to doom

Bending under this awesome weight
seeking a section of eternity
where wisdom is a favored guest
to solve these thoughts inside of me

Why each a copy like I am
of the hand creating him
manipulate and kill his brother
spurred on by a jealous whim?

When God created total man
truly absent of any sin

but silently from far below
he did not see evil sneak in

Someday God Will Stumble Upon Our Burial Ground

With the forest peeking on, in the furrows that
once were sweet to seeds, fallout from war's ashes
fallowed these fertile hills
Come walk with me in the country fields and see
this sickly showing, in the rows nothing growing
and the hungry children looking down wondering
why flowers are not around
These tragic conflicts from brothers hands
achieving destruction across the land
what mindless greedy thinking hath
brought man to this early extinction
Gaining concern from Angels around
reminiscing the billions of years
designing creating the universe
and for mankind a companion station
to enjoy this likeness relation
Loving deeply the race of man
constructed by that holy hand
joggles the reason why this treason
haunting scenes stain this promised land
Poisoned by the hand of man
his planet now completely doomed
times warm memories in bitter ruin
yet God stands stricken, so remembering him

The Residue of Egotism

Truth is vital for survival and
the future of Earth is dependent
on it. Our planet is not a typical
place, the only typical place is the
everlasting night of intergalactic
space.
Earth is indeed a rare and lovely world,
precious in this cosmic darkness.
Our loyalties should be to the care
and preservation of this planet, and
yet, the retarded thrill of war is
prevalent throughout the human race.
Egotistically crippled by thoughts of
supremacy, offensive leaders rush
to conquer and rule pitiful pieces of land,
bound exclusively to earth
But up there in the vastness of creation
a rare perspective awaits us, there are
worlds on which life has never arisen
and others doomed by cosmic catastrophes
We are fortunate, we are alive, the
welfare of our civilization is on our
hands.
The reckless superstition that racism
and violence are the directions needed for
human survival, reeks with an air of
retardation.
No other place in this measureless
universe is there a sphere like earth,
engineered to perfection, single celled
planets evolved, sex was invented, slowly
the ash of stellar alchemy emerged,
gradually life began.
The freedom and direction engineered
for life on earth was not by random
but impeccably equated, each step a
part of the whole with no room for error
And now with the destruction of our forests
and heavy toxic exhausts from
explosive and human
engineered machinery, asphalt
lying where millions of trees

used to grow, our world is now
in grave danger.
There is very little time to put
this planet back in the pristine
condition it was when man was
created, to not, is to suffer the only
alternative, down in our own venomous
waste
It seems strange to insane that
after twenty billion years it had
taken to build us a home,
some retarded groups are hell bent
with their bombs to destroy this
place, this home, that is the only
known planet to house humans

War and Its Casualties

We look back countless centuries and ponder our great
will to survive, struggling from shape to shape
crawling out of the intertidal slime, then
walking boldly upon the earth. For now we are
the embodiment of the universe, we have begun
contemplating our origins and our obligation
to survive is owed to our ancient ancestors.
Welcome to planet Earth, a place of blue skies,
snow white drifting clouds, oceans of clear
water, trickling mountains streams, cool forests
and soft meadows, beautiful and extremely rare.
We live on a tiny fragile world, drifting
in a great cosmic ocean, dotted with trillions
of lovely galaxies and stars. We are fortunate
to be alive. There are worlds that have been
destroyed by cosmic catastrophes, the welfare
of our species is in our hands. To keep this
planet alive and healthy requires constant
planetary untainted care
The human species was finding great success in
colonizing earth when desire to covet land
raised offensive eyes, blind to this lovely
world and the ever unfolding secrets of the
universe, a carnival of engineered
exotic displays, courtesy of the magical stars
Apologies for these satanic behaviors are not
welcome, only pity is felt for these retarded
actors, hell bent on destroying earth and
confounding those who are seeking the hidden
maps of the cosmos, while ignorance, war and
pestilence are ever rewarding to their
sight, culminating in dust from a nuclear war
that would leave the land unable to grow crops
Then the dying screams of hungry children
would be heard down through eternity
We would thus petition that this witless
aggression will not generate the celestial
Angels, to abandon, our earthly gift wrapped home

The Music of the Universe

The sound of April rain is
a song of renewal, awaking
sleeping fields and forests
sprinkling, rebirthing the land

Where once the gentle brush
of heavy winter snow
had glazed these fields
with lullaby like sleepy sounds

Humming winds refashioning
clouds from silent, snowy
wispy white to mysterious
rolling dramatic thunder

Orchestrating from afar
through intervening space the
sun conducts these treasured gifts
in symphonic holy grace

(an in the earth's vast oceans
of water, whale songs range over
great frequencies, while new tunes
appear often, on their HIT PARADE)

A Dangerous Line of Work

It is so noted that it had taken
twenty billion years of risky
construction conditions (exploding
nuclear stars, miscontrolled clashing
satellites, erratic asteroids, meteorite
crashes, shooting stars, etc.)
to create the universe and delightfully
endow us with a home. And now on earth
dangerous trends are in progress
(possession wars, nuclear bomb explosions
guided missiles, pollutants, destruction
of forests, replacing trees with pavement, etc.)
It's as if creation of the universe has
started again, this time on earth
creating a catastrophe instead of another
world.
The climate is warming up to levels
unsafe for man's existence, putting into motion
a plan designed by the creator of the
universe to rid earth's atmosphere of deadly
carbonizing particles and replace the
carbon with beautiful breathable oxygen
by introducing an ICE AGE.
The cost will be in many lives lost
brought on by man's moronic behavior.
Abusing a benevolent gift
When this stage has retreated and the air
is clean with precious oxygen, will man
make the same mistake, with
his pompous ass-inine devotion to greed?

Survival on Planet Earth

Once there was only space, cold dark uninhabited desolate
space, and endless silence when time was not yet recognized,
when evolving molecules began bonding with different atoms
multiplying expanding across this eternal silence, breeding
nuclear molecules throughout this infinite void. Then a
hidden signal in this nameless vacuum released thermonuclear
energy converting hydrogen to helium powerproducing an
extensive monumental nuclear explosion that stretched across
infinity. This, this was the beginning of the universe
and with it a tender parental feeling of creating life,
the coming of man was now unfolding.
Sweeping clouds of interstellar gold hued exotic dust
from this titanic bang began constructing stars and their
accompanying planets and now with light from the stars
gravity was born by way of the distortion of space.
Guiding these many authored wonders is an intangible
particle inhabiting the nucleus of all molecules fueled
by the hand of God devoted to the celestial plan for
a resident universe for each mankind.
When stars spend all their nuclear power they produce
supernova explosions that give birth to siblings born
from these ashes.
The surplus residue from these storms would soon fill
the universe, darkening and disrupting it's countless
duties but gravity from the stars spins and forms
giant black holes that attack, compress, pulverize and
destroy all excessive matter leaving a clean
universe for future expansion. Then slowly from
starlike exotic dust, planet Earth was born into these
intergalactic spaces so desolate that by comparison
a planet is a rare and precious thing.
Even more extraordinary was the star that passed down
through Orion and settled ninety three million
miles from Earth with life producing light
Welcome to planet earth a place of blue nitrogen skies
oceans of water, cool forests, and soft meadows
a little world rippling with life.
Looking out from this rare and beautiful planet, one
can realize earth is the shore of the cosmic ocean
and endless sea of stars and planets, calling,
luring, enticing man to explore
But captivating greed for earth's riches embraced him to

destroy in his quest to dominate and rule the earth
This disappointment was felt across the celestial kingdom and his behavior did not go unnoticed by God, he sent his only son to earth with teachings for global peace needed for the planet's survival
(have compassion for each other and love for the children)
Yet man was lost in his hungry dreams for worldly possessions, he arrested the celestial
visitor with his message, then nailed him to a cross subjecting him to ridicule. Then when nearing death engraved in the stranger's reflective eyes was fatherly forgiveness
(a childlike gift he left behind)
(a childlike gift for all mankind)

A Neighbor in Waiting

The beauty of earth is extended to all to view
but to the observer it is only a tiny part of
the eternal whole, being impossible to digest
the intricate entirety at any one time. I. E.
The universal plan to support humans, animals
and other life is to maintain the right
environment for their existence and yet the lack
of concern for the health of planet earth
is of a moronic nature.

The accumulation of carbon is leading to an
atmospheric catastrophe caused by environmental
pollution. Oxygen is the key to life, without
it the forests will die while the restless wind
and rain try to force carbon into the earth
as part of the plan to save earth.
Then rivers will swell carrying carbon into the
seas in hope of cleansing the skies.
All life on earth is at stake, without livable
habitation no man has a last chance to change his behavior
I. E.
No more wars, everyone knows it's madness, but
hypnotized by mutual mistrust every nation
has an excuse for it. Stop poisoning the
atmosphere by replacing the much needed
tree masses, clean up the seas and limit
human population, for any great increase
will swallow earth's every resource
or, lose our home to troubled neighbors.

In Remembrance
A Cloud of Evil

This colossal feat of tragedy
obliterating the two twin towers
a damnable act by demonic clans
spawned by vile satanic powers

The screams of dying igniting infants
combats exploding flame for space
this burning hell of falling towers
leaves no room for their escape

The killing of children won't go unnoticed
observed critically above from him
in the time worn halls of heaven
God stood stricken, so remembering them

The blood spilled here hardens the air
our land is dealt a terrible deed
but with courage honor and pride
America will wish to rebuild from seed

Warmed by the Wonders of Earth

Waking to fashions of the day
dawn clamoring down the lane
the rising sun scattering night
to witness roses after rain

Assorted hues of wild wind flowers
crisscross the field to bring
life again to winter's folly
in measured time for fussy spring

The metered beat `tween spring and fall
heralds the birth of different flowers
old blossoms sleep while majestically
colorful maple leaves now tower

Under ground a mystic world
awakening roots to disclose
the promised life of mother earth
conspiring with rain to nurse the rose

In these fields of sheer delight
clever earth has a kinship view
with universal rhythm
and the ticking of eternity

As hours laze away to days
days to months months to seasons
I greet each year with courtly grace
and enjoy God's complex reasons

An Internal Review

It's easier to begin a war
than control envious desires
robbing nights of tender sleep
`stead of sharing harmony's fires

Greed, sole impasse to welcome peace
finding housing in an orphaned brain
living a terrible servitude of famine
leaving no chance for life giving rain

Time is life's only dimension
and with love and constant care
man can drown this warlock beast
alerting genocide to beware

Or live in pain and timeless fire
renting the same destructive head
each time man eats he feeds the beast
until his soul and body's dead

www.ingramcontent.com/pod-product-compliance
Lightning Source LLC
Chambersburg PA
CBHW060533100426
42743CB00009B/1512